# Islands of my Life

Judith Davis

Presentation by *BookLeaf Publishing*

Web: www.bookleafpub.com

E-mail: info@bookleafpub.com


ISBN: 9789363317598

First edition 2024

*"Islands of my Life" is dedicated to my dear family, Anne and Jamie, who themselves are also islands of my life for love, for adventure, for my spirit's home.*

# ACKNOWLEDGEMENT

These poems are previously unpublished. The artwork on the covers is original of the poet/artist.

# PREFACE

Islands have always intrigued me, have lured me on their shores, have stolen my heart, have become my spirit's homes, perhaps because even as I docked on their shores, I knew I could not stay forever, but for a time. They have become places of oasis and refuge in the dark nights of my soul, and they have become places of incredible beauty and peace, respite and relaxation. From soaring glaciers to peaceful ponds, from fabulous sunrises and sunsets to quiet bicycle rides along their shores, to refreshing swims in their surrounding oceans and delightful kayaking looking for seabirds, these special islands of my life have given me gifts of peace and rest, of renewal and refreshment, of community and worship, of plein air painting, of fascinating birds and seals and whales and so many of God's creatures, of inspiration for photography and poetry, and most of all, glimpses of my heart's home, even just for a time.

# Bermuda

A cruise to Bermuda was a grand trip to a new island
as we enjoyed the cruise ship and seabirds alongside.
We saw fabulous July Fourth fireworks from land
and our cats were not along on our trip to hide.

Our cabin with a lovely veranda was so sweet
and we often ate our breakfast outside with the birds.
Our son and I saw fabulous seabirds as a treat
and we loved new birds like the red-billed Tropicbird.

Bermuda Audubon's President took us to see
many new birds while our ship docked on shore.
We saw many new species of birds like the Kiskadee,
And we were overjoyed by seeing so many more.

I loved the West Indian Whistling Duck the most
But I also enjoyed a Black-necked Stilt on the coast.

# Block Island, a Spiritual Home

I loved Block Island at first sight in 1990 when I rode my bicycle in an American Lung Association fundraiser.

We rode along the Connecticut coastline for three days, camping at night, and finding our way to Point Judith, a small village in a Rhode Island town where we and our bicycles boarded a ferry for Block Island.

The New Harbor marina welcomed our ship and passengers for our day of riding around Block Island. I loved the island, its pristine, rocky beaches, its beautiful Great Egrets, Great Blue Herons and Laughing gulls. I loved the cliffs at Southeast Lighthouse, Sachem's Pond at the North Lighthouse, and the breezy bicycle ride.

I loved the birds in the water at New Harbor—American Oystercatchers, Bonaparte's Gulls, and Common Eiders. I also loved seeing Common Loons, and White-winged Scoters and three species of gulls.

I loved the many sailboats and kayaks at Old Harbor and wanted to kayak. I loved the clam fritters and Del's Lemonade we enjoyed at Rebecca's Take-out in New Harbor, and I loved riding along Spring Street and seeing St. Anne's-by-the-Sea Episcopal Church, that I would later serve.

Block Island became the spiritual island home of my life for twenty years, and I was always sad to leave it.

# Celia Thaxter's Garden on Appledore Island

Growing up in North Carolina, I had never heard of the New England poet Celia Thaxter of Appledore Island. In late August, 2010, I attended a watercolor workshop in the Isles of Shoals off the coast of Kittery, Maine.

We stayed on Star Island in the vintage Oceanic Hotel from the grand days of 19th century Victorian hotels. Every morning, we painted *en plein air* around Star Island imaging rocks, clapboard cottages, and flowers.

One day we took a boat to Appledore Island where Celia Thaxter lived and hosted artist salons in the 19th century. Her close friends Childe Hassam, Nathaniel Hawthorne, and Sarah Orne Jewett attended her salons in summer.

Ralph Waldo Emerson and William Morris Hunt were also inspired by Celia Thaxter's island home. Like Hassam, we painted outdoors in her garden, still maintained by those who love Celia Thaxter's flowers.

I painted Corn Poppies, Hollyhocks, Delphiniums, and so many beautiful flowers that Childe Hassam painted there. Foxgloves, Dahlias, Sweet Peas, Snowdrops, and varieties of poppies lent color to Hassam's paintings. Hollyhocks spread down to the rocky water's edge and brilliant Rose-colored Iceland poppies color the garden.

I loved painting in Celia's garden and I loved reading her poems as well, both inspiring my love of art and poetry. Every summer I stay on Star Island and visit Appledore Island and Celia's Garden and give thanks for her gifts.

# Epistolary for Star Island

Dear Star Island,

I fell in love with you more than a dozen years ago when the steamship docked on your rugged shore. The sweet smell of your beach plums filled my head and heart with joy.

The lovely dawn chorus of the Yellow Warblers and Common Yellowthroats brightened my morning. Your beautiful Spotted Sandpiper showed me her chicks near the East rocks, and I remember well your poet Celia Thaxter wrote a lovely poem about the Spotted Sandpiper.

I have loved so many of your birds over the years—American Oystercatchers, Black Guillemots, Common Eiders and Common Terns, and yet none of them is common to me, but wonderful.

I savor every, every minute I'm on Star Island and wish I could stay forever, falling asleep to the gentle sounds of the bell buoy and foghorn and waking at "0-dark thirty" with the brilliant sunrise shining in my window in the old, Victorian, Oceanic Hotel.

When our steamship sails to the mainland from the Isles of Shoals, gentle tears flow down my cheeks as I pray to all that is holy that I will come back.

Love, Judith

# Far-Flung Islands

I

Far-flung islands, the Isles of Shoals, rose in view ten miles out in the Gulf of Maine.

I sailed aboard the S. S. Thomas Leighton from Portsmouth to Star Island.

Why do islands, fragile, distant, lonely, seem like home?

II

Isles of Shoals, ten miles out, became a home, and reminded me of the phrase in *The Book of Common Prayer*, "this fragile earth, our island home."

As the Leighton docked at the end of the pier on Star Island, the college student summer staff, the "Pelicans" chanted to us from the dock, "You did come back, you did come back," and Old Shoalers aboard chanted back, "We did come back, we did come back."

III

Star Island greets me every June now and for more than a dozen years, has filled me because of limited time, brief encounters, fledgling birds.

When the Leighton docks, I want to run down the gangplank and hug the whole island.

I sketch island scenes, draft poems, savor sunrise and sunset, and love every Common Tern and Yellow Warbler.

When the sun sets behind the "Summer House", I breathe salt air.

The huge orange ball pops up from the sea's horizon every morning.

IV

Appledore Island's sunrise comes at 04:30 as I look across from Star Island.

I read Celia Thaxter's poem "The Sandpiper" again and again. Spotted Sandpiper comes out to greet me from the rocky ledge of Star.

I search for her fuzzy chicks nesting on the rocks.

V

We sail over to Appledore Island to see Celia Thaxter's garden of Blue Cloud Larkspur, Corn Poppies, Delphinium, and Wild Scarlet Pimpernel.

I come to see the Black Guillemot seabirds and nesting gulls with chicks. Barn Swallows build their nests near the porch lights of the Oceanic Hotel;

every summer I watch them fledge as Tree Swallows take up residence in the Bluebird houses.

VI

I walk to the chapel at night, with my hurricane candle lantern, to lead worship.

I savor the taste of a Lime Rickey, coffee ice cream, and Swedish Fish from the snack bar.

I buy a new T-shirt, coffee mug, or copy of Celia Thaxter's poems.

As I board the Leighton again, I cry when the "Pelicans" chant their song to us "You will come back, you will come back!"

# Fledglings on Star Island one Summer

Barn Swallows are ready to fledge.
Mama birds feed them all the time.
Their nest is under the porch roof of Cottage C.
One fledgling fell from the nest and died just before it
would fly and be free.
I was heartbroken for that little life--snuffed out like the
chapel hurricane candle lanterns.

'Nature's way,' some say, which does not help my grief.
A Gray Catbird flew into Newton Hall in the Stone
Village.
It went to the window and sat on the lower sash-- trying to
find a way through the glass.
"Just fly down and go out the open window," I said, But it
didn't understand.

Panicked, it kept fighting. Gently I placed my hand over it
and then set it free.
Holding that precious little life blessed me that day.
It lost four tail feathers as it flew to a nearby bush, yet it
was free to fly, unlike the Barn Swallow fledgling.

Death and Resurrection, the cycle of life!
I will never forget the Star Island Barn Swallows and
Gray Catbirds, Spotted Sandpipers, Yellow Warblers,
Eider ducklings (only one this year), and Black
Guillemots, Terns, gull chicks, and Red-winged
Blackbirds. Stay safe, little Star friends until I see you
next summer. I love you always, little feathered friends.

# Invitation to Birdwatching

Please accept this invitation to join me birdwatching, Not in my backyard, but out on trails and the lake at the nature preserve. Many of your feathered friends will join us for our morning walk. I issued invitations to them as well.

Spring suggests it might arrive anytime now. I heard the peepers last evening. Birds are already carrying nesting material. I saw the elegant Great Blue Heron hurrying to the rookery with a twig in its bill.

High overhead I saw the Bald Eagle carrying a twig. The Great Horned Owl has already accepted my invitation. Now she sits on her nest high in the bare tree and it's just mid-February. She is sitting on eggs and lifts her ear tufts so I can catch a glimpse of her.

Songbirds seem to be pairing up now like the herons and owls and eagles have. I saw a pair of Eastern Towhees on the ground. Several Eastern Bluebirds sit on the power line. Tiny Ruby-crowned Kinglets dart back and forth in trees.

Song Sparrows and Swamp Sparrows hop around the boardwalks. I heard a Virginia Rail in the marsh; that's rare for February. Migration is always a delightful surprise as I dust off my binoculars once more. Will you join me in Spring's delight?

# Island Beach Birds

With great delight, I drove across the causeway to the small island.

Brown Pelicans flew in formation low over the ocean. Royal Terns darted back and forth over the waves. Busy Sanderlings ran around the surf looking for supper.

Great Black-backed Gull caught a Spider Crab. My heart soared with joy to feel the cool water on my bare feet and the gentle breeze in my hair after so long.

Brown Pelicans and Laughing Gulls, my friends. The ocean, my happy place.

The warm sun and sand, my cheerleaders, The sound of surf, gulls, and terns, my choir. The rhythm of the waves, my muse The beach, my happy home.

# Island Feathered Friends

A song I had never heard came wafting from the wetland on Block Island behind the vicarage.

Looking into the marsh, I saw him perched on the reeds, displaying his brilliant red epaulets.

Someone said his name was Red-winged Blackbird, but I didn't know bird names then.

The Red-winged, my "spark" bird made me a birder.

I sought birds on the islands of my life from then on--Bear Island, Bermuda, Block Island, Cape Cod, Cuttyhunk, Hispaniola, Hog Island, Star Island, and Vancouver Island.

A King Rail called from the marsh on Bear Island.

A Red-billed Tropicbird soared near me in Bermuda.

A  Ring-necked Pheasant visited me on Block Island.

A Black-capped Chickadee ate seeds from my hands on Cape Cod.

A Warbling Vireo sang to me on Cuttyhunk. A Magnificent Frigatebird loomed large on Hispaniola.

A Black Guillemot swam near me off Hog Island. A Spotted Sandpiper showed me her chicks on Star Island.

A Rhinoceros Auklet teased me on Vancouver Island.

A Red-winged Blackbird sang to me as I sang "Morning has broken. . .Blackbird has spoken like the first bird."

# Islands of my Life

1
What was the first island of my life?
When did I first go to an island?
What islands stole my heart?
I went to Roanoke Island in 1960.
I went to Long Island in 1968.
I went to Great Britain in 1968.
I went to Ocracoke Island in 1975.
I went to Key West in 1988.
I went to Elsinore in 1988.
I went to Block Island in 1990.
I went to Prudence Island in 1992.
I went to Aquidneck Island in 1992.
I went to Newfoundland in 1992.
I went to the Island of Børnhølm in 2002.
I went to Cuttyhunk Island in 2009.
I went to Martha's Vineyard in 2010.
I went to Star Island in 2010.
I went to Appledore Island in 2010.
I went to Nantucket in 2010.
I went to Vancouver Island in 1995 and 2014.
I went to Bermuda in 2015.
But which of these islands stole my heart?

2
Block Island became a spiritual home from 1990 to 2013.
I lived there for six weeks in the winter of 1995.


I loved its rugged shore, its beaches, its lighthouses, its
seals and birds.
I loved the Episcopal Church community I served for
many years.
I painted a few watercolors of the rocks and the Church.

The Danish island of Børnhølm was a place of joy
with-my art class in 2002.
My class painted there for ten days that summer.
I loved skinny dipping in the cool island ocean. I loved
attending the Lutheran Church even though I didn't
understand Danish.
We painted *en plein air* for ten days at Annegreta's
and Jerker's farm.

Star Island became my new spirit's home in 2010.
The steamship SS Thomas Leighton from Portsmouth, NH
took me to Star Island.
I loved the cool water, the rugged shore, the sound of the
foghorn and bell buoy.
I loved attending chapel at night with hurricane candle
lanterns.
I painted watercolors there for a whole week in a Road
Scholar conference.

Our family cruise to some Alaska islands was in 2014.
The Holland American ship was luxurious, and our
adventures were awesome.

I loved the seabirds and whales--Horned and Tufted
Puffins, Auklets, and Orcas.
I loved worshipping on the beautiful ocean surrounded by
glaciers.
I did watercolor sketches in my journal every day we were
in Alaska.
I first loved Vancouver Island in 1995 when I visited
friends there.
In 2014 I spent several days in Tofino and the Pacific Rim
National Park.
I loved the pelagic birding trip with my son as we saw
Murres, Razorbills, and Puffins.
I loved worshipping in the Redwood Cathedral with
incredibly tall Redwoods.
I painted watercolors of our days in my sketchbook
journal.

# The Jetty at Red River Beach

The jetty at Red River Beach was their favorite fishing
spot.
"Let's go to the beach," the boy said to his Mama, and off
they all went.
Low tide waves barely reached the rocks of the jetty, and
his Mama handed him the baited fishing pole.
As soon as he cast the line, a few fish nibbled at the bait.
He was overjoyed as the fish pulled the line.
His Mama helped him reel in the fish, which was too
small to keep.
His Mommy, not on the jetty, walked along the shore
picking up a few sea scallop shells and gathering seaweed
as great compost for the garden.
Warm late afternoon sun warmed them to stay awhile,
hoping for a nice catch as they stood on the rocks.
His Mommy walked close to the jetty as a few waves
broke the top of the rocks.
His fishhook got stuck on the moss on the rocks and he
was afraid to stoop down to unhook it.
His Mama said she would get it free and she bent down to
reach the fishhook.
Then he saw his Mama fall hitting her head on the rocks.
He screamed "Mommy!" who heard him from the beach.
Just as the ambulance arrived, he said, "But what about
my fishing pole?"

# Kanasgowa
# [KAH-na-SKOE-wa]: Heron

My herons on Cape Cod, how I will miss you as I move to
the Cherokee country of the Western North Carolina
mountains.

The Cherokee named you Kanasgowa, the Heron.
We looked at a house to buy on Kanasgowa Lane, and
how I would have loved to live on "your" street.

One autumn, almost a decade ago, we migrated north to
Cape Cod, and now we will migrate south—you to the
shores and salt marshes, and I, to the mountain lakes.

I will look for you on the lakes as I long to see you again:
You, my favorite, majestic one, the Great Blue
Heron—You, the diminutive Little Blue Heron— And
you, the visiting Tri-colored Heron that made me smile as
I added you to my "life list"--

You, the elusive one, the Green Heron with several colors
in the spring, yellow near your eyes, green and maroon on
your wings

—And you herons of dusk I watch flying to your roosting
trees—Black-crowned and Yellow-crowned Night Herons.

We have enjoyed the quiet of the salt marsh—you, fishing
for supper, and I, chilling out with you.
You, flying to your roost at dusk, I, counting you for my
"year list."

I will miss our peaceful, quiet times in the evening by the
beaches and marshes of Cape Cod, and I wish us blessings
as we migrate to our new homes.

You will migrate back to Cape Cod next spring, and I will
wait patiently for your return to our mountain lakes, for
you, Kanasgowa, will always be in my heart.

# Once you have slept on an Island

Rachel Field authored a poem about sleeping on an island in Maine the late 1930's.

I read her poem in the early 1990's, but its meaning eluded me until I had slept on an island in Maine.

Sleeping on an island has a special kind of magic and leaves an imprint like no other experience.

Our small group of nature sketchers boarded a boat in Port Clyde for Monhegan Island one June morning in 2014.

Wesaw an Atlantic Puffin on the ocean alongside our boat and our hearts soared with joy.

We loved our island inn, The Trailing Yew, a vintage set of Maine cabins that took us back in time.

I stayed in the Seagull Cabin with fabulous views of the surrounding ocean and its variety of gulls.

I slept to the sounds of gulls, bell buoys, and foghorns, all lulling me to sleep and then waking me up at dawn's first light.

Rachel Field said it best of our experience, that even when we left this great island adventure, we would continue to "see blue water and wheeling gulls wherever our feet may go."

We sketched images of nature around the island for a long weekend, and we ate delicious seafood and went birdwatching with our naturalist leader.

While I did not see any "life birds" that weekend, I saw
wonderful birds like Sooty Shearwaters, Wilson's Storm
Petrels, and Great Shearwaters, all birds that live at sea.

We loved our time of sleeping on that island, sketching its
rocky shore and seabirds, and then we understood what
Rachel Field wrote in her poem: "once you have slept on
an island you'll never be quite the same!"

# Pink Peonies

Pink Peonies outside the door of the stone cottage on
Star Island were like cotton candy,

The kind sold at the pre-Fourth-of-July Carnival in
Bristol, Rhode Island the evening before the historic
parade along Hope Street whose center line had
been painted red, white, and blue,

The kind Mama wouldn't let us buy because it was
pure sugar,

The kind that was pale pink and blue on a stick and
yummy.

Yummy, but fleeting in taste and substance, and
longed for anyway.

The pink Peonies were fleeting, too, their lush, large
blossoms fading in the hot sun, beaten down by rain, but
longed for in summer and enjoyed oh, so
briefly like this lovely and fleeting journey of life,
and the few days on Star Island every summer.

# Prudence Island

Prudence Island, or Hog Island, is very small
and lies less than a mile from Bristol, Rhode Island.

The small ferry boat can take one car at a time to haul
and a few passengers who walk on from the land.

We could see Prudence from the State Street dock
just behind my workplace, St. Michael's Church.

Whenever the time struck three on St. Michael's
Clock we knew to head to the ferry just beyond a tree of
Birch.

Once I spent a night on the island listening to the
foghorn and the bell buoy making sweet sounds as I slept.

Once you have slept on an island you will always
mourn for those days and sunrises at early dawn as they
crept.

Wakened by the sun shining brightly at dawn's first
light, we were excited to have another day in our special
place.

Island days go too quickly and our souls delight
with each moment being thankful for this grace.

# Saying Goodbye to the Great Egret

The Great Egret soared like a Bald Eagle high
overhead at Red River Beach.

The setting sun illuminated its yellow pointed bill
like a flashing dagger.

When I walked along the shore the next morning, the
Great Egret stood like a striking silhouette against the
bright morning sun.

The blinding sun shone like diamonds on the water at
the egret's feet as it watched for the quick move of the
crayfish that would be breakfast.

When I watched the egret stab the crayfish, I stood
like a statue, and did not even raise my camera as I
honored the egret's beauty and presence.

The fiery sun, dancing on the still water, called both
of us to pause and give thanks for our time together.

When fall migration begins, I will move from my
favorite beach on Cape Cod to the mountains of North
Carolina, soaring in my mind like the egret, grieving in
my heart to lose this precious communion.

I will miss my egret and our quiet times of stillness in
my spirit's island home of Cape Cod.

When I look for other egrets soaring over my new
lakes and ponds, my heart will leap with joy like a child
when I see them gliding beautifully in my new home.

However, I will miss this egret and our harbor of

peace on Cape Cod, our anchorage, our island home.

One day I hope to return to Cape Cod seeking lost
treasure, homecoming with my egret.

For now, this stunning Great Egret in its white robe
will soar in my heart and quell my grief until we meet
again.

# Sonnet for an Island in Denmark

One July day when the weather was warm
we Capitol Hill friends set sail to paint
at our Danish friend's historic farm
on Børnhølm, the Danish island so quaint.

Our watercolor teacher from Capitol Hill
went with us on this art adventure to teach
and to enjoy this Scandinavian thrill
and paint in all the places we could reach.

Each day we painted outdoors near the shore
And shared our paintings at night.
I love that watercolor sketchbook more and more.
I cherish our adventure and all the sights.

Our flight home from Copenhagen was bittersweet
because our grand painting adventure was a treat.

# Spotted Sandpiper of Appledore Island

Celia Laighton Thaxter grew up in the Isles of Shoals
off the coasts of New Hampshire and Maine in the
mid-to-late 19th century.

Mostly unknown to southerners, she was not only a
fabulous poet, but an artist as well, and part of the
Transcendentalist movement in New England.

Her literary friends were Nathaniel Hawthorne,
Henry David Thoreau and Ralph Waldo Emerson, along
with Sarah Orne Jewett and Annie Adams Fields.

Her artist friends were Childe Hassam, William
Morris Hunt, and Rose Lamb.

Celia grew outraged by the slaughter of birds for
ladies' hats, which she called "funeral pyres they carry on
their heads," and she loved the birds of the Isles
of Shoals.

She is remembered as a famous author for "Among
the Isles of Shoals," and "An Island Garden," but I
remember her for her poem "The Sandpiper."

My favorite birds on Appledore Island and Star
Island are the Spotted Sandpipers and their summer
chicks.

Celia loved her Sandpiper friend as she wrote,
"Across the lonely beach we flit,
One little sandpiper and I."

Her poem ends with these fabulous words: "For are
we not God's children both, Thou, little sandpiper, and I?"

Every summer on Star Island when the beautiful
Spotted Sandpiper shows me her chicks out near the East
Rocks with a view of White Island Lighthouse,
my heart is happy and I give thanks for Celia
Thaxter's sandpiper.

# Star Island Duplex

I first laid eyes on you as our ship neared Star's
vintage New England Victorian hotel.

Vintage Oceanic Hotel invites
New visitors to Star for their first time.

Many new visitors disembarked today
To begin new adventures on the island.
New adventures on island include birding
and watching Spotted Sandpipers and Common
Terns.

Spotted Sandpipers watch me and guard their chicks.
I love all the new fledglings on my island.

All the new fledglings include Barn Swallows
Waiting for a tasty meal brought my Mama.

# Trinity of Star Island Birds

I
As the S. S. Thomas Leighton steamed out of
Portsmouth Harbor, a cheer went up, because we were
finally headed to Star Island, our spirits' home in the Isles
of Shoals.

Two years had passed with COVID shutdown since
we saw our Star Island birds.
Common Terns and Herring Gulls flew alongside our
boat as we welcomed their presence.

Red-winged Blackbird sang his welcome song as we
docked at the Star Island pier.

"Shoalers" chanted their welcome song--"You did
come back, you did come back!"

We passengers chanted with immense joy, "We did
come back, we did come back!"

Sensing being back at "home," we wanted to kiss the
holy ground of Star Island.

II
Filling our coffee mugs at dawn, we intrepid birders
set out to find our island bird friends.

Our old familiar friends sang to us--Common
Yellowthroat Warbler, Gray Catbird,
Song Sparrow, and Yellow Warbler.

Chipping Sparrows chirped along with Northern
Cardinals and Cedar Waxwings.
Herring Gulls and Great Black-backed Gulls guarded
their nests on the rocks east of the Summer House, but
allowed us a glimpse of their fuzzy chicks.

Faithful Barn Swallows built their nests under the
rafters of the porches of the cottages.

Tree Swallows assumed residence in the nest boxes
and flew in and out to feed their nestlings.

iii
Spotted Sandpiper landed near us on the rocks on our
last day on Star. Our hearts leapt with joy for our reunion.

Black Guillemot swam in the harbor and we thought
we had missed it this summer.

Female Common Eiders started a nursery school for a
dozen ducklings near rocks below Oceanic Hotel.

As the S. S. Thomas Leighton departed Star Island
for "America," our tears welled up again to leave our
birds and a few human friends on the Island.

Joyfully, yet tearfully those of us on the boat chanted
back to the Shoalers on Island, "We will come back! We
will come back!"

# Vancouver Island

A Divinity School friend invited me to Vancouver
Island where her parents had retired a few years earlier.

I was thrilled to visit a new place and island in my
life and to have a grand adventure like none other.

We flew into Seattle and took a ferry to Victoria, that
quaint city that transported me to an earlier time.

We took a water taxi to have had High Tea at the
Empress Hotel with her mom on a grand adventure.

Butchart Gardens had lush greens and colorful
Blooms that longed to be in one of my paintings.

I had never seen so many varieties of roses in one
place. And I loved the Himalayan Blue Poppies.

The Shinto Gate welcomed us to the Japanese Garden
while the Dragon Fountain welcomed us as well.

The Coast Salish style Totems reminded us of
Indigenous Peoples who first lived on the Island.

We drove to the Pacific Rim National Park near
Tofino, a quaint village that seemed to be a place time
forgot.

I bought a soft, stuffed Sea Otter toy in Ucluelet to
remember our great trip to Vancouver Island.